HOW CAN WE KNOW THE WAY?

HOW CAN WE KNOW THE WAY?

Reflections on Belief, Salvation
and Eternal Life

BARKLEY S. THOMPSON

Foreword by Kate Moorehead Carroll
Afterword by Jay B. McDaniel

How Can We Know The Way?
Copyright © 2023 by Barkley S. Thompson

All rights reserved

No part of this publication may be reproduced in any form or by any electronic or mechanical means, including information storage and retrieval devices or systems, without prior written permission of the copyright owner, except that brief passages may be quoted for reviews.

Paperback ISBN: 979-8-8229-2145-0

Unless otherwise noted, scripture quotations are from New Revised Standard Version Bible, copyright © 1989 National Council of the Churches of Christ in the United States of America. Used by permission. All rights reserved worldwide.

Where noted, scripture quotations are from the ESV® Bible (The Holy Bible, English Standard Version®), copyright © 2001 by Crossway, a publishing ministry of Good News Publishers. Used by permission. All rights reserved. The ESV text may not be quoted in any publication made available to the public by a Creative Commons license. The ESV may not be translated in whole or in part into any other language.

Charleston, SC
www.PalmettoPublishing.com

"I in them and you in me, that they may become perfectly one, so that the world may know that you sent me and loved them even as you loved me."

John 17:23, ESV

For the parishioners of

Saint Mark's Episcopal Church

Little Rock, Arkansas

Table of Contents

Foreword xi

Preface xv

Those who believe in me 1

How can we know the way? 23

Where is Jesus? 45

A Reflection on Calling 65

Afterword 87

About the Author 91

Foreword

In every generation, there are a few great preachers. They stand out like lights in the darkness. Their sermons are not just made up of good stories or a charismatic delivery; they actually express a fresh idea—something that you have never conceived of before. These sermons say something *new*, something that unveils a simple yet elegant solution. They take a theological tangle and unwrap it before our very eyes, so that, for the first time ever, it makes sense.

Barkley Thompson is one of these preachers. In the ensuing pages, he tackles some of the greatest "sticking points" of the Christian faith. What does it mean to say that Jesus is The Way? What exactly does it mean to believe in Jesus? And how in the world are we to understand the concept of eternal life?

This small book is a force to be reckoned with. And sometimes, the greatest insights are best expressed simply and in small bites.

The Very Reverend Kate Moorehead Carroll, author of *Vital Signs of Faith: Finding Health in Your Spiritual Life*
Pentecost 2023

Preface

As the old saw goes, "We make plans and the Holy Spirit laughs." Sometimes the opposite holds true. We go about our lives in seemingly random fashion, while the Holy Spirit renders order out of chaos. I have always resisted planning sermon series, because, as an Episcopal priest, I am a dedicated lectionary preacher. I preach what the weekly lectionary gives me, and each sermon stands on its own. So, I was surprised on a Sunday morning last spring when a parishioner said in the receiving line after church, "I've thoroughly enjoyed your current sermon series."

"What are you talking about?" I genuinely inquired. He proceeded with great accuracy to detail for me three sermons I had preached in a row (interrupted by Palm Sunday and Easter) in which I had focused on the questions "What does it mean to believe in Jesus?", "What is salvation?", and "What do we mean by eternal life?" To his ears, these sermons were all of a piece, an intentional progression of theological thought.

Though there was no conscious intention to connect these homilies thematically, my parishioner was obviously correct. He went on to suggest that the sermons, taken together, could serve as the basis for a group study wrestling with these seminal Christian questions. That suggestion and encouragement led to the present monograph, in which I have taken the homilies and morphed them into reflections for prayer and discussion.

The final reflection in the book is much more personal. It was delivered at the 2023 Urban-Suburban Clergy Conference, of which I've been privileged to be a member for the past decade. It was also written and delivered unwittingly in the middle of the other reflections in this collection. Rereading it, I realized that it embodies the theology of the other reflections in my daily living over the course of two extremely challenging years.

I wish to thank the good people of Saint Mark's Episcopal Church, among whom I have yet to serve for long, for embracing me so whole-heartedly as their rector and for their willingness to grapple theologically and desire to know

God intimately. I also thank my friend and fellow priest Kate Moorehead Carroll for providing the foreword and my mentor Jay McDaniel for penning the afterword. Both are prolific authors whose work flows from their own deep wellspring of faith. I give thanks finally and always to Jill, who loves me more than I deserve and with whom, by God's grace, we have built a life I love.

For those for whom questions of belief, salvation, and eternal life have seemed too difficult to explore; for those who have been abused by the answers of a punitive and otherworldly Christianity; and for those just now beginning to seek a deeper meaning to life, I pray this little book is a helpmate.

Those who believe in me

John 11:1-45

If one is fortunate in life, at least once or twice she will encounter someone whose vision, passion, dedication, and charisma capture her imagination and her heart. She will find herself setting aside, or at least suspending for a time, her own goals and intentions and putting herself in service to that figure who has inspired her. Importantly, such a following is not slavish and unquestioning. A truly inspiring leader does not attempt to squelch questions or critique. But even so, inspiring leaders exude an infectious desire to do right and do well, to further some virtuous goal with verve and passion. If you have ever encountered such a person—if you have ever *followed* such a person—you know what I am talking about. And if you have not, you will know it when it happens.

I have encountered such a person. He is Ellis Arnold, the current president of my alma mater, Hendrix College. In his long and illustrious career of leadership, Ellis has served as president of three institutions, and his achievements unquestionably now mark him as an elder statesman of education (though, in truth, he is not that old). But I first came to know Ellis when I was a twenty-one-year-old Hendrix College student, and he was a thirty-six-years-young Hendrix vice-president already evidencing the talent that would lead to his rise. A few years later, when I was twenty-five and Ellis was forty-one, Ellis served as president of a university in Tennessee, and he hired me to be his director of admissions. We worked closely side-by-side for two years before I left to go to seminary, and I have never had an experience like it, before or since.

Ellis articulated a vision for the university that was hopeful and necessary. When he spoke about it, Ellis lit up, even at times when he was otherwise weary. Ellis labored for the college harder than anyone else around him, and his dedication made those around him want to work harder and more faithfully, too. In those years, Ellis was not flawless. He would occasionally second-guess, or misstep, or move too quickly for others. But his humanity simply made us want to follow with greater dedication, not less. Though it seems strange to say so, Ellis was the embodiment of the vision and the hope he pursued—he lived and breathed it—and that is what inspired the rest of us. That is what inspired me. At the end of the day, the best and perhaps only way to say it is that I *believed* in Ellis Arnold, and I followed where he led.

John 11:1-45 is the story of the death of Lazarus, the only individual in John's Gospel who is referred to as Jesus' friend. There is so much in this story to plumb, but I want to focus on Jesus' statement right in the middle of the passage—the statement that often perks one's ears and reclaims one's attention—because it is at the same time one of the most cherished *and* the most divisive statements in the Gospels. Here it is: "Jesus said to her, 'I am the resurrection and the life. Those who believe in me, even though they die, will live, and everyone who lives and believes in me will never die.'"

We read these words at the beginning of every Episcopal funeral service. In that setting, they are words of profound comfort, with the promise that life has not ended, but changed. Thank God for them. But in other settings, marked less by grief than argument, these same words become lines in the sand, dividers, even litmus tests. "Whoever believes in me will never die," Jesus declares, and then asks, "Do you believe this?" And that presents the rub. What does it mean to believe in Jesus?

For the past several centuries, especially in American Christianity, the answer has leaned toward "beliefs," with an "s" on the end. And by beliefs we mean propositions about Jesus that are claimed to be factually true. A good example is the literal virgin birth, but there are plenty of others. "Believing in Jesus" is generally taken to mean that you assent to the laundry list of propositions. You affirm them, whatever they are, as literal fact, and if you can check all the boxes, then you believe in Jesus. And thank God that you do, since checking those boxes is what is required to inherit eternal life. By the same token, beware if you cannot in good conscience check all the boxes, because eternal life depends on it.

Is that depiction of belief in Jesus familiar to you? For those who grew up in evangelical and fundamentalist churches, it almost certainly is. And such a primary understanding of belief can create intense anxiety, guilt, and despair of salvation if, internally and deep down, we harbor doubts and aren't so confident of our intellectual assent.

An example: During my seminary summer of hospital chaplaincy, I had a patient who had suffered a stroke and was experiencing aphasia. He was unable to understand or form complete, coherent sentences. His wife was desperately afraid of her husband's damnation because he had never declared propositional belief in Jesus, so she wanted me, as the chaplain, to go into his room and encourage him to speak after me, word for word, "I believe in Jesus Christ as my personal Lord and Savior." As if assenting to that formula aloud was some sort of magical incantation that made all the difference; as if that is what belief in Jesus means.

Hear me say: It isn't. Jesus' birth, life, death, and resurrection are surely wondrous. In Jesus, God did something cosmic and unique. But our assent to any particular dogmatic articulation of how to understand God's action in Jesus is *not* what John—or Jesus—means by belief.

The first thing we need to notice, in this and all the great "I am" statements in John, is that Jesus is likely not even referring to himself in the first part of the statement. Remember, "I Am" is the first and proper name that God gives to Godself way back in Exodus. At the burning bush, Moses asks God who God is, and God says, "I Am."[1] So, when Jesus says, "I Am the resurrection and the life" he's not saying "*I, Jesus,* am the resurrection and the life." Jesus is actually saying, "God, the 'I Am,' is the resurrection and the life." If we misunderstand that, we misunderstand the rest. That is Jesus' vision. That is the Way, the Gospel he wants us to understand: that *God* is resurrection; *God* is life.

---

[1] Exodus 3:14

To believe in Jesus is not to say or affirm all the right things *about* Jesus. Remember how I described young Ellis Arnold at the outset. Believing in Ellis didn't mean that I affirmed facts *about* Ellis: that he grew up in Little Rock, has a law degree, or likes to bird hunt. When I said I believed in Ellis, I meant that Ellis inspired me. I caught his vision, trusted it, gave myself over to it, and followed him towards it.

Amplify that cosmically, and we come to understand what it means to believe in Jesus. It means we give ourselves over in trust—heart, mind, body, and soul—to the vision of God that Jesus embodies in his words, his life, his death, and his ultimate resurrection. *That* is what it means to believe!

A story like the raising of Lazarus, in which Jesus doubts himself not once, but twice, in which Jesus expresses deep grief and sorrow, and in which Jesus expresses the profound power of God, inspires like nothing else. The passage ends by saying that those who walked with Jesus and experienced all of this *believed in him*. Not things *about* him. Not propositions. Jesus spoke and lived the vision that God—the great I Am—is resurrection and life, and Jesus' own fulsome trust in that vision inspired others to trust and follow. It was contagious.

It still is. As disciples of Jesus, we are invited to give ourselves over to that vision completely, Will Jesus inspire us? Will we trust him? Will we believe in Jesus enough to follow him and live into his vision of God? If we can, then we will experience resurrection and life.

Questions for Reflection

1. If you were raised in a church, how did you understand what it meant to believe? In what ways was such a notion of belief challenging for you?

2. What is the difference between beliefs and the kind of belief described in the reflection?

3. If Jesus is referring to God in his "I Am" statements, how does that

change the way you envision who Jesus is?

4. Is it easier or more difficult to believe in a Jesus who doubts, second-guesses, and grieves?

How can we know the way?

John 14:1-14

John 14:1-14 always reminds me of the story of the Episcopalian who dies and meets Jesus at the front door of heaven. "Come right in," Jesus says cheerfully, "In my Father's house there are many rooms. Let me show you around." As the two walk down a long hallway, the Episcopalian glances in an open door to see a jazz band playing and scores of people dancing with wild abandon.

"Who are they?" the Episcopalian asks. "They are members of the Church of Christ," Jesus says, "They were not allowed to play musical instruments or dance on earth, so here they get to cut loose."

As Jesus and the Episcopalian walk a bit farther, they pass a room with an Olympic-sized swimming pool with water slides and diving boards and filled with scantily-clad swimmers drinking fruity rum drinks. Everyone is having a great time. "And who are they?" the Episcopalian asks. "Those are the Southern Baptists," Jesus replies. They were not allowed to swim or drink in life, so now they get to have their day in the sun, so to speak."

As they continue down the hallway, the revelry quiets until things are so still all that can be heard is a slow, repeated creaking coming from the final door. As they approach, the new arrival can see a room filled with near-catatonic people in rocking chairs, hands folded in their laps, rocking back and forth. The man asks, "And who are these?"

"These are the Episcopalians," Jesus answers. "They got to do everything on earth, so they don't get to do anything up here!" (Makes the Episcopalian reader just a little bit nervous, doesn't it?)

John 14:1-14 is the single most frequently chosen scripture passage read at funerals. In the hundreds of funerals at which I have officiated over the past two decades, I estimate that this passage has been read 90% of the time. Why is that? Because, on the face of it, it seems to be all about the *destination*. It is all about where we go when we die, about what is at the other end of that long, opaque tunnel we can ultimately and only travel alone. It serves as an assurance to us, and for those whose loss we grieve, that whatever is beyond that tunnel will be good.

In a first century world in which the house of virtually anyone less than nobility would have consisted of one or two small rooms[2], Jesus paints a picture of a spacious home—or, as the *King*

---

[2] See, for instance, St. Peter's house in Capernaum on the banks of the Sea of Galilee.

James Version puts it, a mansion—with many rooms. And one of those rooms is prepared for *you*. That's a wonderful comfort.

Notice why: The image Jesus' audience receives is one from their own fantasies and daydreams of maximal comfort and ease. Heaven consists, in other words, of what we wish *this* life were like. Our images of heaven are not a lot different than those of the joke I relayed at the outset. Whatever we wanted life to be in the here and now but wasn't, that's what heaven *will be.*

It has always been so in religions and cultures that have a conception of an afterlife. For the Greeks, heaven was the Elysian Fields, the place heroes and the chosen go upon death, described by Homer as, "where life is easiest for men. No snow is there, nor heavy storm, nor rain, but ever does [the] ocean send up the…west wind that [it] may cool men."[3] The Greek poet Hesiod adds that Elysium is populated by "happy heroes for whom the grain-giving earth bears honey-sweet fruit."[4] Sounds pretty good, doesn't it?

In Islam, the Quran describes heaven similarly. Heaven, it says, consists of "gardens of lasting bliss graced with flowing streams." Those in heaven "will be adorned with bracelets of gold. They

---

[3] Homer, *Odyssey* (4.560-565)
[4] Hesiod, *Works and Days* (170)

will wear green garments of fine silk and brocade [and] be comfortably seated on soft chairs."[5]

I love such images. But here is the thing: They all draw the attention away from life and toward death. They constantly look past the present to a future beyond knowing.

Even more important is this: In the Gospels, Jesus is recorded as speaking over thirty-one thousand words. By the

---

[5] Quran, Surah 18:31

best count, he speaks of heaven exactly twice.[6] What does this tell us? It reveals that our common, conventional understanding of Christianity—that it is primarily about our path to heaven—is wrong. That is not to say heaven does not exist. But it is to say that we have allowed our own insecurity, anxiety, and fear about what happens after we

---

[6] Obliquely in the Parable of Lazarus and the Rich Man (Luke 16:19-31) and directly on the cross in Luke 23:43, when Jesus says to the thief, "Truly, today you will be with me in paradise."

die to coopt a Gospel message that is almost entirely about *something else.*

Let me put it this way: There are religious billboards throughout the American South that pose in huge, ominous letters, "Are you ready to die today?" That always seems to me the wrong question. A better, more faithful Gospel question would be, "Are you ready to *live* today?"

How might we read this Gospel passage from John differently if we understood Jesus to be talking about not the way to where we go when we die, but the way to live in the here and now? You see, Thomas does not ask Jesus, "How can we know the *destination*?" Thomas asks, "How can we know *the Way*?" That term is loaded with meaning in the Gospels and in early Christianity. Indeed, in the Book of Acts, the followers of Jesus are primarily referred to as "People of the Way."[7]

---

[7] See Acts 9:1-2.

Jesus' original followers understood, in ways we have lost, that the Christian life—the life of discipleship—is not about where we go when we die, but how we live.

At the risk of getting a bit esoteric, I want to introduce you to my favorite early church theologian, a fellow named Origen who lived in the early third century A.D. Origen's careful study of the creation stories in Genesis—those first three chapters of the bible that tell us about how we were created and how we fell from grace—revealed to him that Genesis uses two different verbs for how we were created.[8] The first word, from Genesis 1:27, is the word from which we derive our English word "poetry." The second word, from Genesis 2:7, is the word from which

---

[8] "Flesh and Fire: Reincarnation and Universal Salvation in the Early Church," by Charles Stang. Harvard Divinity School, 2019, https://hds.harvard.edu/news/2019/03/19/flesh-and-fire-reincarnation-and-universal-salvation-early-church, (accessed May 3, 2023).

we derive our English word "plastic." Origen argued, in effect, that God originally created us as God's own poetry. (Isn't that a great image?) But as we ignored God, grace, and goodness and fell farther and farther from God, we hardened, and became less like poetry and more like plastic. We became locked into our rigid, worldly ways of being and forget how to be poetry in this world at all.

If we take Origen's theology seriously (and I take it very seriously), then the Way of Jesus—the message and call of Jesus upon our lives—is to become poetry again in this world. Through joy, celebration, worship, fellowship, embrace of the marginalized, and service (especially through service) we begin to lose our rigidity like the Tin Man in *The Wizard of Oz* when oil is added to his joints. We shed our plastic coating and begin to be fluid with grace. Like the words of Shakespeare, Wendell Berry, Mary Oliver, or Amanda Gorman, we once again become poetry in this world.

And what is more, the point is not to be this way *until we get to where we are going when we die*. The Way is not the path *to* heaven. The Way *is* heaven. Jesus is not saying to Thomas today, "When you die, you will get there." Jesus is saying, "The Way I have been teaching you and showing you and exemplifying for you *is the destination*. The Way *is* Truth and *is* Life."

Put differently, if we follow the Way of Jesus, all of life is heaven. If we do not, then we miss heaven entirely.[9] If we fail to follow the Way of Jesus, we remain rigid, plastic things. If we follow the Way, we become the very poetry of God. Are you ready to *live* today?

---

[9] This is a rough paraphrase of C.S. Lewis in his preface to *The Great Divorce*.

Questions for Reflection

1. How do you imagine heaven? Have you ever considered where your conception of heaven comes from?
2. Does focusing on the afterlife improve or impair the way you live?
3. What does the Way of Jesus mean to you? What does it look like to follow the Way?
4. Are Origen's images of plastic and poetry helpful? What would it look

like for you to be God's poetry in the world?

Where is Jesus?

Acts 1:6-14, John 17:1-11

He wears a red and white-striped sweater. Regardless of the temperature, he is never spied (when he is spied at all) without his toboggan cap. I am told he wears glasses. Since 1987, people have been searching far and wide for him: straining, squinting, trying to catch a glimpse. Whether in a crowded city scene, on the beach, or at the circus, we struggle in vain to detect his presence. Until sooner or later someone cries out, "Where's Waldo?"

My wife and I read the Waldo books to our kids when they were little. They would turn each page with glee to hunt for Waldo, but as their eyes scanned up and down to no avail, smiles would be replaced by furrowed brows, as the toboggan cap and striped sweater remained elusive. And if the kids were tired and cranky, the whole enterprise would end in tears.

In Acts 1:6-14, Jesus leaves the disciples and, in Luke's telling, literally ascends into heaven like some god in a Greek drama, as if hoisted into the sky by pulleys and ropes. Just before Jesus disappears, the disciples ask him, "Lord, is this the time when you will restore the kingdom to Israel?" The language in which the question is cast is opaque to us, but they are asking, in essence, "Now that Easter has happened—now that you have defeated death—is this the moment when wounds will be healed, brokenness mended, wrongs righted? Is this the final scene when all of God's purposes will be fulfilled?"

In response, Jesus equivocates. He says, "It is not for you to know the times or periods that the Father has set by his own authority." And with that, like the Wizard of Oz rising into the sky in his hot air balloon, Jesus is gone.

From that moment to this, the followers of Jesus have been waiting and looking. We want Jesus to return to finish what he started. And while each generation tends to think it lives in the midst of the very worst the world can get, it is true that our own present world is thoroughly broken. Whether we consider war and devastation in far flung places like Sudan or Ukraine, the hunger we see each week right here at Saint Mark's through our food pantry, natural disasters such as the recent tornado that affected so many in Little Rock[10], or the toxic polarization of relationships throughout communities across the globe, the project of redemption and repair Jesus began surely seems unfinished. If we are so inclined, we might borrow the words from Peter's

---

[10] On March 31, 2023, a tornado ripped through central Little Rock, Arkansas damaging or destroying hundreds of homes.

first letter and say, "Like a roaring lion, our adversary the devil prowls around, looking for someone to devour."[11]

All of which begs the question, where *is* Jesus? What is he doing? When will he appear? Where will we find him? Is he up in some ethereal heaven, looking down on us like the Greek gods on Olympus, or is he hiding in our midst, like Waldo in those children's books?

---

[11] 1 Peter 5:8

As we strain our eyes to see him, we can certainly sometimes meltdown like children in our confusion and sorrow, as Jesus remains hidden from us in our hurting world. What, then, to do? With Jesus that elusive, how do we direct our anxiety in his absence?

In the previous reflections in this book, we have considered how some modern strands of Christianity have coped with Jesus' absence. They turn faith into a binary dualism, focusing not on this life but on the *after*life. In reaction to the furtive, subconscious anxiety that Jesus is missing altogether, they posit instead that Jesus is up there in that faraway heaven where he rose on those ropes and pulleys so long ago, and that the entire point of this life is to focus on our individual status as either eventually joining him there or being cast into hell.

Could that be what it is all about? Let us turn to the 17th chapter of

John's Gospel and find out. I love John's Gospel, but it is by far the most difficult of the four gospels to preach, because in it Jesus delivers extensive speeches on the nature of God and us, or—as in John 17—engages in lengthy one-sided conversations with God the Father. When Jesus' thoughts are broken into bite-sized bits, as John's Gospel tends to be when preached or studied in bible studies, the bits can be taken to mean anything we want them to mean and not at all what Jesus intends. Consequently, John's Gospel is notoriously easy to misunderstand, both by lay people and, frankly, by preachers.

Take, for example, the idea of "eternal life," which is the emphasis of John 17:1-11. Because of the tendency I described above, when, in our desperation to find Jesus we dilute Christianity into being primarily the means by which we will eventually get to join the disappeared Jesus up there in heaven, we take the term "eternal life" and, in our minds if not in our words, we automatically translate it to mean "afterlife." But that's not what John means by eternal life at all.

Which gets us back to our search for Jesus. Where is he? Throughout John's Gospel, read as a whole and not in bits, we get a completely different sense of what Jesus' ascension might mean. Absent in John are Luke's images of a Jesus lifted up into the clouds. Rather,

Jesus' many speeches and prayers in John instead talk of a union between God and Jesus' followers that is accomplished in and through Jesus. It comes to a head in 17:23, where Jesus prays to God, "I in them and you in me, that they may become perfectly one, so that the world may know that you sent me and loved them even as you loved me."[12] Just a few verses prior at 17:3, Jesus gives a name to this union.

---

[12] English Standard Version

He says, "This *is* eternal life, that [my followers] may know you." It's no secret that, in biblical parlance, the term "to know" means more than data points. It means an intimate knowing, like that of lovers, an embracing union.

The biblical scholar William Countryman wrote a book called *The Mystical Way in the Fourth Gospel*[13], and that title may help us to understand

---

[13] Countryman, L. William. *The Mystical Way in the Fourth Gospel: Crossing Over Into God*, Trinity Press International, 1995.

what Jesus is talking about more than anything else. Eternal life is *not* the afterlife. It does not refer to us rising up to heaven to join the Jesus who got there before us. It means that, somehow, Jesus has *already* joined us to God *mystically*. Somehow, through his resurrection, just as the temple curtain was rent open, Jesus has opened our souls, and into us Jesus has flowed, like the current of a river. Jesus has not ascended *up there*, John says, but *in here*.

And that presence of Christ in us, connecting us directly to the divine—to God—replaces the life we have lived with a new life, *eternal* life, the life in which God is not, even now, distant and apart from us, but *in us*, uniting us with God and with one another. "I in them and you in me," Jesus says.

Where is Jesus? We can quit straining our eyes to look for him, hidden in the crowd. We can stop pining for the day after death when we will finally rise up to meet him. Jesus is right here, right now. Jesus lives in you and in me, and through us. Jesus is a risen, living reality. If we look inwardly for him, into our own souls, our anxiety will melt as we meet Jesus there. And we will find ourselves empowered by his presence to move through the world, binding its wounds and mending its brokenness. When we discover that Christ lives within—truly lives, connecting us to God—then eternal life begins this very day.

Questions for Reflection

1. Does Acts' depiction of Jesus' ascension make sense to you?
2. Is it difficult for you to find Jesus in today's world? Where do you look for him?
3. Have you always understood eternal life to refer to the afterlife? Is it liberating to consider that eternal life means something else?

4. How does it affect your faith to imagine that Jesus' ascension means he has entered into us and connected us to God in a new way?

A Reflection on Calling

John 3:1-15

I am going to break every homiletic rule this morning[14] and acknowledge that this reflection is, in many ways, all about me. That said, I hope it is all

---

[14] This reflection was first delivered at the Urban-Suburban Clergy Conference in Memphis, Tennessee, on April 18, 2023.

about you, too. In two months, I will have been ordained twenty years. The last two of those twenty have presented me with greater physical challenge and more angst than this already-angsty priest would have thought possible. Things are much better now, but my recent experience, most especially weeks upon weeks during which I was mostly lying flat on my back, gave me protracted pause for reflection on what was, and what is.

In the 2017 indie film *First Reformed*, Ethan Hawke plays the Reverend Ernst Toller, a clericals-wearing minister who serves the two hundred-fifty-year-old colonial First Reformed Church. Ernst is a damaged and conflicted soul who determines to keep a prayer journal for one year as an attempt to tease sense from his torment. Much of the film consists of Ernst moving through the motions of his days, with the internal monologue of the journal playing on screen. That monologue is largely a consideration of calling. In one among many memorable scenes, Ernst writes, "Discernment intersects with Christian life at every moment. Discernment: Listening and waiting for God's wish what action must be taken." Immediately after these lofty, highbrow, and true words, the camera shows Ernst pouring Drano into the church toilet and going to work furiously with a plunger to unstop a clog. It is a great juxtaposition.

I still remember the first time I put on clericals. Just before seminary graduation, I had purchased a black, long-sleeved clergy shirt and collar. I put them on, sat at the edge of the bed in our little Austin rental house on Harris Park Blvd., and stared at myself in the bedroom mirror. Though I was still a few weeks away from my diaconal ordination, I thought I sensed, for the first time, what Professor Bill Adams meant when he spoke of the ontological change that comes with ordination. Like Peter Parker bitten by that radioactive spider or Clark Kent bathed for the first time in the light of our yellow sun, I felt as if something in me was—or was about to be—*different*. I should also acknowledge that as a teenager I was a prolific reader of comic books, and a therapist would no doubt have a field day analyzing my lifelong desire to wear costumes and play superhero.

I was ordained in Memphis, Tennessee at age thirty, and I immediately fell in with a small cadre of other youngish, new priests who sat in the back at clericus, rolled our eyes at our older colleagues at clergy conference, and generally believed that the ails of the church were due to the laziness and ineptitude of its priests. We called our group Goya, which we told others derived from the Hebrew *Goyim*—the people—but which was really an acronym, G.O.Y.A., standing for Get Off Your Ass, our indictment of our fellow clergy. I am pretty sure we were insufferable.

Despite our attitudinal deficits, our intention was true. We—I—believed that the grace and power of God would redeem this good earth, and I believed with only slightly less fervor that through my own relentless hard work and dogged will, I could bend the world in God's direction. Sort of like a superhero.

A few years ago in Santa Fe, Kayleen Asbo taught our colleague group Dante's *Divine Comedy*, leading us through hell to heaven, and the following summer I took it upon myself to study Dante in greater depth. That resulted in a Dean's Hour series I taught at Christ Church Cathedral in Houston entitled, "The Way Down is

The Way Up," and both the study and the course title proved prescient for my own life.

In February of 2021, I was diagnosed with prostate cancer, a rare thing for a forty-eight-year-old man, and as proved to be true in my case, a more aggressive cancer when manifest in the forties. No sooner had I recovered from cancer surgery than a lumbar spine that had been deteriorating for more than a decade finally gave out, and three back surgeries later I ended up with a tear in the lining of my spinal cord and a spinal fluid leak. That leak caused "brain sag," which resulted in persistent headaches more intense than I knew possible. The only relief came from equalizing the pressure in my head and spine, and the only way to do that was to lie flat. Which I did for five months, including one week in neurological ICU and twenty-three full days on my back.

During the past two years, I first shed my pretense of invincibility, then my pretense to be able to bend the world to my will, then the pretense of just being o.k. I experienced guilt, fear, depression, and finally despair. I was on the way down, but I did not see how that trajectory could ever be the way up.

The way down began to be the way up in late October last year, when I was able to visit the Mayo Clinic. Good counsel, good medicine, and time have allowed me to adjust to a life that is different, a life with some chronic pain and some limitations, but that is now, strangely, fuller and richer than it has ever been before. It is a life in which I now think back on that scene in *First Reformed*, and I am taken less by Ernst's lofty words about discernment and more by the plunger in the toilet. Or, better said, the plunger in the toilet gives new meaning to Ernst's words:

"Discernment intersects with Christian life at *every* moment. Discernment: *Listening* and *waiting* for God's wish what action must be taken."

At some point in each of our lives, we discerned that God and the Church were calling us to the priesthood. And, as I have gleaned from our annual conversations, we continue to discern all the time whether or not God *still* calls us to the priesthood. As for me, I do not really like to wear clericals anymore. I wear a collar as seldom as possible. Not because I reject my ordination—God's calling is more palpable to me than ever—but because the notion that priesthood is somehow like the bite of a radioactive spider is now so completely foreign to me. Priesthood, for me, is now about plunging clogged toilets, and in the best way.

In *First Reformed*, Ernst's journal, reflecting further on calling, reads, "Some are called for their gregariousness. Some are called for their suffering. Others are called for their loneliness. They are called by God because, through the vessel of communication, they can reach out and hold beating hearts in their hands. They are called because of their all-consuming knowledge of the emptiness of all things that can only be filled by the presence of our savior."

I believe that today as profoundly as I believe anything. As I skirted despair the last couple of years, there was nothing left but Jesus. As my physical being betrayed me, the only way to arrest the spiritual downward spiral was to look to Jesus and hope Jesus would pull me up. Lest I preach an entire homily without a nod to the Gospel text, this is my story of Nicodemus approaching Jesus under cover of night and slowly coming to grips that the emptiness of things can only be filled by the presence of the savior. In *First Reformed*,

Ernst Toller says, "Reason provides no answers…Wisdom is holding two contradictory truths in our minds simultaneously. Hope and despair. A life without despair is a life without hope. Holding these two ideas in our heads is life itself."

That *is* priesthood, I now believe: Holding up the hope of the savior in the face of despair. If we think we are about anything other than that, then we are merely putting on costumes, at worst playing superhero and at best playing parts that are for others to play. We plunge toilets. We unclog spirits. We hold up hope. We speak of the savior. We hold beating hearts in our hands. What a privilege. What a gift.

Questions for Reflection

1. Have you ever worried that God was calling you to be a superhero? What did that look like in your life? How did it work out?
2. What experiences have you had in your life that have altered your understanding of God's call?
3. What might it mean to say that God calls us to plunge toilets?

4. What would it look like to hold up hope in the face of despair in your life?

Afterword

I needed this book. Often, we Christians think of Christianity as having beliefs about Jesus and other high-minded matters. Christianity becomes, for us, a matter of believing the right things, whatever "right" means to us. *How Can We Know the Way?* presents very differently: as a way of living, filled with truth and life, in which Jesus is present, not as someone about whom we have propositional beliefs, but in whose Way we participate whatever the circumstances of our lives. Christianity becomes a verb, not a noun. We find Jesus in the world, in our lives, in the circumstances at hand, and in how we respond to them—in honesty, hope, and, of course, love. The beauty of this book is its coalescence of form and content; the way the Way becomes real to us, not through didactic sermonizing, but through stories, images, and Barkley Thompson's own sharing spirit. After reading this book, the first thing you want to say is "Thank you." The next thing you want to do is to share it with others so that they, too, can better walk the Way.

Jay B. McDaniel
Professor of World Religions, Emeritus, Hendrix College

About the Author

The Reverend Barkley S. Thompson serves as rector of Saint Mark's Episcopal Church in Little Rock, Arkansas. Previously he served parishes in Collierville, Tennessee and Roanoke, Virginia, and for ten years he was the dean of Christ Church Cathedral in Houston, Texas. Barkley holds a Bachelor of Arts in Philosophy

& Religion from Hendrix College, a Master of Arts in Religious Studies from the University of Chicago Divinity School, and a Master of Divinity from the Seminary of the Southwest. He is the author of *Elements of Grace and In the Midst of the City: The Gospel and God's Politics*, which won a Gold Medal Illumination Award and a Silver Medal IPPY Award. Barkley is married to Jill, and they have two grown children.

www.ingramcontent.com/pod-product-compliance
Lightning Source LLC
LaVergne TN
LVHW092053060526
838201LV00047B/1372